THE ULTIMATE
WIN/WIN

THE ULTIMATE WIN/WIN

Communicating Love
to Your Family
(Including Your Teenagers)

TARGUM/FELDHEIM

First published 2000/5760
Copyright © 2000 by Moshe Goldberger
P.O. Box 82
Staten Island, N.Y. 10309
Tel. 718-948-2548
ISBN: 1-56871-168-9

Published by: **Targum Press Inc.**
22700 W. Eleven Mile Rd.
Southfield, Mich. 48034
targum@netvision.net.il
Fax: 888-298-9992

Distributed by: **Feldheim Publishers**
200 Airport Executive Park
Nanuet, N.Y. 10954
www.feldheim.com

Printed in Israel

This sefer is lovingly dedicated
in memory of our father and grandfather

Chaim (Hyman) ben Zev HaCohen Lemberg

3 Nissan 5756

whose attributes
of loyalty, unselfishness, honesty,
and love for his family
shall always be an inspiration.

The Lemberg Family

With thanks to:

Rabbi Eliezer Gevirtz
Rabbi Menachem Goldman
Mordechai Gelber
Yitzchok E. Gold
Binyomin Siegel
Simcha Kagan
Charles Mamiye
Daniel Lemberg
and
a special thank you to
C.B. Kaganoff
for all your help.

Contents

Preface

The welfare of your family is a Torah priority of the highest magnitude. The family unit is the foundation of a person and of society as a whole. One of our greatest challenges in serving Hashem is treating others properly.

The quality time you spend with your spouse, your children, and your parents will be one of the most rewarding investments of your life.

We need to learn how and why to make our families a priority in our lives.

It is essential that a home becomes a center of kindliness where the husband, the wife, and all of the children endeavor to always make each other happy. Since a person has many more interactions with his family than he has with other people, these opportunities for success or failure are most frequent.

"Who is wealthy? He who rejoices with his portion" (*Avos* 4:1). A person's family is a great part of
his portion in life. Hashem has provided you with
your specific set of parents, your siblings, your
spouse, and your children. Take some time to think
about all of these people regularly and to rejoice
over them. Express gratitude to Hashem daily for
the wealth He has bestowed upon you.

"How beautiful are your tents, O Yaakov, your
dwellings Yisrael" (Bemidbar 24:5). Building a Jewish home requires wisdom and effort. "The wise
woman [and man] builds her [his] home" (Mishlei
14:1). The home is the training ground for developing kindliness, responsibility, patience, humility, loyalty, industry, selflessness, and similar character
traits of excellence in oneself. It takes the combined
desire, energy, talents, vision, and determination of
both parents. It takes time, thought, planning, and
prioritizing.

When we set out to improve our communication with our families, we may have to also focus on
changing ingrained negative attitudes such as
"There's no way I will ever make something out of

myself" or "I can never get along with so-and-so. We are too different." Both of these attitudes must be uprooted if you want a pleasant family life.

The Mishnah instructs, "Do not consider yourself inferior" (*Avos* 2:13). Review this message a hundred times until you believe it in your mind and heart. You can do whatever you set out to do, with Hashem's help. Getting along with certain family members may be difficult because of their personalities, but it can be done if you put thought and effort into it!

When you focus on the thoughts, "I can do it with Hashem's help" and "I am important, because Hashem created me with great potential," you will find that you have the energy and the ambition to succeed.

Ask yourself a few simple questions.

❖ Do you interact with, or at least talk to, each of your children daily?

❖ When you do spend time with your children, are you totally there?

❖ A wise person is always learning from every person

(*Avos* 4:1). Have you learned lessons by observing and listening to each of your children?

❖ Does your tone when you speak to your spouse and children sound more cheerful and understanding than it does when you're speaking to your friends?

If you answered no to any of these questions, we suggest that you make this book into a family handbook to serve as a springboard for discussion and application. It will take many readings until these ideas become integrated into your personality, but it will happen more quickly and effectively if every point is shared, step by step, with family members. When you learn together, you will have the opportunity to spend time together, learn from one another, and practice improved methods of communication together.

The lessons we are presenting are not our own suggestions. They are all ideas that you can observe in life and discover from the words of our Sages. Our purpose here is to set up a framework with the Torah's guidelines that will enable you to apply these lessons to your own unique situation.

Chapter One

Clarify Your Goals

The Ramchal in *Mesilas Yesharim* teaches us that the foundation of self-perfection is clarifying our purpose in this world. We need a clear and compelling vision of what we stand for and what our family stands for. When you know your destination, you can make each decision along the way with clarity. Knowing your goal gives you the drive and determination you need to succeed. With power and purpose, you can rise above trials and tribulations and do what really matters most.

> *The world stands on three pillars: Torah, service, and kindness.*

> (*Avos* 1:2)

This statement of the Mishnah is the foundation of every Jewish home. It has to be at the forefront of our consciousness at all times. Pause right now and ask yourself:

❖ What is my purpose in life?

❖ What are my methods for accomplishing that purpose?

❖ What are my family's goals?

❖ What is my goal in marriage?

❖ What are our highest priorities?

The overriding goal in our lives is to fulfill Hashem's Torah. We are responsible and accountable for the way we handle everything in life, including interpersonal relationships. By learning Torah, we stay focused on our goals and we acquire the tools to deal with and resolve all of life's challenges.

Through Torah, we develop and maintain our ongoing relationship with Hashem. In addition, we have an obligation to develop positive relationships with people. With our family especially, we need to learn to share, communicate, enjoy each other's company, and serve Hashem together. How do we accomplish this?

One key to instilling Torah values in ourselves

and in our families is to repeat to yourself the lessons of the Mishnah and Gemara. When a husband and wife internalize Torah statements and train their children to repeat them as well, the lessons become the family's way of life.

People need a sense of their values and vision in life. With a sense of family identity and purpose, we can reach great heights in serving Hashem and dealing with people.

As times passes, we need to update, redefine, and reaffirm our life's mission. As our children grow older and our family changes, our family's goals will also need readjusting. Each member of a family has unique talents and abilities that have to be taken into consideration in developing, adjusting, and fine-tuning a family's mission.

It is important to learn how to deal with the individuals in our lives and with their needs. There are numerous *mishnayos* throughout *Avos* that teach specific applications of the *middos* and qualities that we need to focus on.

Your home should become a place of nurturing, support, encouragement, happiness, honesty, respect, kindness, patience, and discipline.

The more we focus on these details in a practi-cal, concrete way, the easier it becomes to make our commitments real. When you have a clear set of rules and principles that you are focused on, you can hold onto them. "When you grab a small amount, you will succeed" (*Chagigah* 17a). Keep your goals in mind constantly and live your life by them.

As in all areas of Torah, review is essential. Imagine, for example, a family reviewing this type of a message at their Shabbos table: "We are always going to help each other. We will pray for each other daily. We will not hold any grudges against each other. We will forgive each other and always love each other." These are all obvious mitzvos, but verbalizing them will help you relate to them in a concrete way.

Mesilas Yesharim starts off with the concept that the more obvious things are, the more we tend to disregard them and eventually forget about them. The remedy to this is to keep reviewing and focus-ing on the issues.

Recognize that maintaining a peaceful atmosphere in your home is one of your main priorities. The Torah teaches us that we must treat every person with love and respect. If you are not a mensch at home, all of your other accomplishments will be artificial, superficial, and fallacious. You need to make sure your focus is always on your priorities — fulfilling the Torah and mitzvos in every aspect, and especially in the home.

Chapter Two

The Family Unit

The concept of the family unit was designed and created by Hashem. This helps us realize how essential it is. Some of our happiest moments in life are spent with or result from our families.

"Everything in this world is a test" (*Mesilas Yesharim*, ch. 1). Every situation in life is a challenge, but the greatest challenges provide the most opportunity for growth. One of the biggest ongoing struggles is maintaining a peaceful home — we need to work hard physically and emotionally. At the same time, though, we grow, we refine ourselves, we learn to enjoy life more, and we are fulfilled. "According to the difficulty, so is the reward" (*Avos* 5:23). Keep in mind that Hashem has placed every one of your family members into your orbit to test you for your ultimate benefit.

When we develop the attitude that the time we spend with a family member is an opportunity and a test from Hashem, we learn to savor the moments, instead of thinking we'd rather be someplace else. True success in life is garnered by developing personal perfection through dealing with the people and the situations Hashem sends our way.

We are given specific mitzvos to perform for our family members. For example, we must honor, love, and revere our parents, teach Torah to our children, and respect and honor our spouses.

As a husband and wife purify themselves, the Shechinah resides with their union.

(*Sotah* 17a)

When a husband and wife unite to serve Hashem with mutual respect, love, peace, and harmony, Hashem joins their union. This is the foundation of the Torah approach to the family unit, which serves as the setting for the service of Hashem. In order for children to grow up happy and well-adjusted, it is essential for their parents to understand them and for them to be taught to understand their parents. This is only possible when there is understanding and communication between the father and mother themselves.

Ask yourself, "Am I a good listener?" Listening to others is part of the great mitzvah of *chesed*. Do you seek out and value opinions other than your own? Can you listen to someone else and put yourself into his or her shoes? Do you "love your fellow Jew as yourself" (Vayikra 19:18)?

This fundamental mitzvah, to love one another, includes the basic principle to respect others and their feelings. Sometimes, when we are busy, it is hard to take the time to be sympathetic to our spouses and children. Still, we must recall that one of our biggest jobs in life is to make our family members happy.

Your children will pick up on your feelings for them from your behavior.

* ❖ When you recognize your children — they feel worthwhile.
* ❖ When you approve of them — they are proud of themselves.
* ❖ When you are friendly to them — they are happy.

A person has a great responsibility to his family members, the Talmud teaches, based on the verse, "Do not hide yourself from your flesh [i.e., your relatives]" (Yeshayah 58:7). You are responsible for providing friendship, food, clothing, warmth, and good cheer for your family.

A good time to do this is at the Shabbos table, when we have built-in family time that can be utilized in many ways. Shabbos is a time for communicating, having fun together, bonding through attentive listening, and learning about one another through sharing what is important to each of you.

Each family member has to be treated as a star. Let every child shine. Let them feel that all of the others appreciate their unique input.

If your family's Shabbos meals do not reflect these ideas, it is time for you to change and improve the situation. By paying attention to the needs of each of the people in the room, you can transform the atmosphere into a more loving, peaceful, and harmonious one. Your example and leadership will help change your entire family. Although every family situation is unique, you can learn the necessary principles and how to apply them to your situation.

We can use *Mesilas Yesharim's* Torah definition of true love to summarize the general atmosphere of an ideal Jewish home. There are three components to true love:

1. *Simchah* — to enjoy spending time together.

2. *Deveikus* — to share beliefs and values and to interact with each other.

3. *Kana'us* — to defend the honor and respect that is due to each other.

(Mesilas Yesharim, ch.19)

It takes great efforts to develop, apply, and perfect these Torah ideals, but the joy and satisfaction that result are well worth the effort. Even when family members are very different, with different interests and talents, they can learn to respect and appreciate each other.

Every person has unique talents, strengths, and interests. Some people are very creative and enjoy writing or drawing. Some people enjoy learning and intellectual pursuits, while others have greater social skills.

When people develop their unique talents and

do the things they enjoy, they find it exhilarating. A person's confidence and self-esteem is built this way. Hashem has implanted these special talents and inclinations in each person, and they should be appreciated, utilized, and developed. If you and your family members use your God-given talents properly, you will be able to enrich your life immensely. Allow each person to become who he wants to be.

The sons of Yaakov Avinu serve as role models.

There was an individual who always loved the seashore.... They discovered he was a descendant of Zevulun. There was a fellow who always insisted on strict justice. They discovered he was [descended] from Dan" (Pesachim 4a). Each brother was different in many ways. This variety enabled each to contribute to the perfection of the entire nation, much as the various organs of one's body contribute to its general welfare.

(*Sing, You Righteous*, p. 338)

In addition to having different strengths, we also have different weaknesses. When a family recognizes each person's weakness and works to accommodate this, everyone benefits. We can balance each other out by focusing on each person's strengths, and caring for and sharing with one another.

A healthy family grows stronger over the years by the ongoing balancing and developing mutual trust and respect for one another. A family also grows when it overcomes trials together.

When you sit at your Shabbos table, take a few moments to appreciate each member of your family. Think of each person's unique capabilities, and pray for them that they should have a great Shabbos, both physically and spiritually, which will give them renewed vigor for the coming week. They should all be inspired to love each other more and to relate to Torah and mitzvos with enthusiasm and joy.

Just a few moments of quiet reflection about your children and spouse will make a world of difference in your interactions with them in the coming week. Remember that you love them and want to treat them accordingly. Remember that every family member serves as an avenue of opportunity for your own personal achievement.

Chapter Three

Communicating Love

Wat are the most important mitzvos of the Torah?

We all know that loving Hashem is one of the greatest mitzvos. Another similarly great mitzvah, which parallels the love of Hashem, and is actually a form of loving Hashem, is the mitzvah of loving your fellow Jew. Hillel taught that this mitzvah is the summary of the entire Torah (*Shabbos* 31a).

Although we tend to think of love as an emotion, it is important to realize that it must be practiced in actions as well. We need to always treat others, especially our family members, the way we would want to be treated ourselves.

The very first *mishnah* in *Avos* teaches a fundamental approach to dealing with all aspects of life. "Be patient in making decisions" (*Avos* 1:1).

Hashem has granted us a gift — the ability to choose how to respond to every situation. Practicing love for our family members entails behaving toward them with patience, understanding, and consideration. We can choose not to react rashly when pressured. We can choose to stop and think things over before reacting.

A person can sometimes lose his whole future by failing to stop and think before acting. One prime example of this is Reuvein, the son of Yaakov Avinu. He lost his birthright, as Yaakov told him, "Because you were hasty as water" (Bereishis 49:4). Think of this metaphor when you turn on a water faucet. Water flows freely, but we have to be in control. Our minds have to be put into gear before we open our mouths, before we take action. The more we practice this skill, the better we become at using it.

One of the foundations of patience is the mitzvah to love every Jew and thereby be sensitive to his needs. Some parents forget that this applies to their children, as well. They criticize, scold, and judge their children without thinking about the children's feelings. Siblings may also sometimes continually quarrel and bicker with one another. What can be done to alleviate and rectify this problem?

We can utilize "pause" power. Stop and think before you open your mouth to criticize or express disapproval. Your family doesn't deserve to be snapped at all the time. Appreciate the good that they do for you and talk to them in a kind and warm tone of voice. Even if someone speaks to us in anger, we should learn to respond with a gentle answer, which will diminish anger (see Mishlei 15:1). We can learn to discuss problems and differences without frustration or annoyance.

To refrain from speaking impulsively, learn to be aware of your ego and pride. If we focus on others instead of only on ourselves, we will not lose our tempers and yell at our spouse or children as much.

Do not be victimized by your evil inclination. Control your temper and do not explode when problems arise, as they inevitably will. Analyze the situation and find a solution that will work for you. If you raise your voice at someone, you have given in to your ego. You create tension and lose the character perfection you would have garnered had you remained calm instead. (For more on this subject, please see our book *Guard Your Anger* [Southfield: Targum/Feldheim, 1999].)

Occasionally people who mean well act in erroneous and harmful ways. For example, a man, accustomed to debating issues with his *chavrusa* in yeshivah, spoke in a similar manner with his wife whenever she tried to discuss any issue with him. However, his aggressive debating tactics intimidated his wife. Unlike his *chavrusa*, she thought her husband was angry at her and became agitated by what she perceived as his lack of sensitivity for her. "Why do you explode at me all the time?" she would ask miserably.

This husband had to become aware of his wife's distress and train himself to communicate with her more gently. Understandably, it was difficult, but nonetheless it was essential in order to obtain and maintain a happy family life. He had to stop thinking about justifying himself and satisfying his ego. Every person must realize that his goal is promoting his home's peace and harmony.

When the home is a place of enthusiasm for Shabbos and all other mitzvos, no child will ever break away. This tragedy is only possible if the joy of serving Hashem is lacking because the mitzvos are performed mechanically, in a dry manner.... A Jewish home should constantly be brimming with the joys of Torah Judaism. There is no complaining or worry, only strength and joy.

(Rabbi Avigdor Miller, *Awake My Glory*, p. 353, 355)

The voice of song and salvation is always found in the tents of the righteous.

(Tehillim 118:15)

Children should be taught optimism, confidence, and happiness so that they will always view the world in this manner and serve Hashem with joy all their years.

(Rabbi Avigdor Miller, *Awake My Glory*, p. 371)

Our job as parents is to make the atmosphere of the home. We must choose to speak with kindness and love always, and, better yet, to demonstrate kindness, patience, and respect to others at all times.

When children are demanding or your spouse

fails to show you the proper respect, it is sometimes hard to maintain a loving tone of voice. In a tense situation, use your sense of humor. Cracking a joke can diffuse a lot of anger and help everyone view the difficult situation through a new light.

Hashem wants us to always serve Him with joy and happiness (see Tehillim, ch. 100). Spending time with your family can always be enjoyable if you choose to make it that way. Kosher humor is positive and uplifting, a relief from pain and tension.

Love your fellow Jew as yourself.

(Vayikra 19:18)

Love is a verb. It is based on a decision. Interact with your family members in a positive way to create a pleasant and happy relationship with them. It does take work, but it will be worth it.

Realize that no mitzvah is beyond your capability. You may feel it is too difficult to be always calm and even-tempered, but that is not true. You are not a helpless victim of your evil inclination; you can perform this great mitzvah. Hashem is instructing you to take the initiative to love every family member without exception and to manifest this love through support and kind words.

A husband is instructed to honor his wife even more than his own body (*Yevamos* 62b). This is an important concept that must be kept in mind if a husband wants to maintain a strong, healthy, growing relationship. He will try not to say anything that may cause hurt feelings, he will apologize when necessary, and he will remember that winning an argument is not always the best thing. What is more important in life, being right and having things your way, or being kind, giving, forgiving, and doing the best thing for the entire family?

Loving Your Teenager

Ask yourself: "Do I 'greet every person with a pleasant countenance' (*Avos* 1:14) when I interact with my teenager?" There are always things you can do to improve your relationship with your teenager.

The great Sage Rabban Yochanan ben Zakai would enumerate the praises of his five great disciples (*Avos* 2:8). The Rambam teaches us that the mitzvah to love every Jew obligates us to relate their praises (*Hilchos Dei'os* 6:3). This is a mitzvah we must practice — loving our teenagers for at least one specific quality that they possess.

Are you always criticizing, blaming, and battling wills with your teenage son or daughter? Think for a minute how you would feel if you were on the receiving end of all that criticism and blame. Although it is not always easy to get along with teenagers, the Torah still commands us to love them — and act on that love.

When you inquire of your teenager, "How are you?" make sure to do it with warmth and real caring. Every person has a need to be loved and every person has an obligation to love the other people involved in their lives. It takes effort to demonstrate and develop one's love on a daily basis for another person, but the results will show and be worth the investment.

It also takes effort to refrain from constant criticism. Without realizing it, we tend to criticize teenagers for numerous things, such as what they eat, what they wear, what time they wake up and what time they go to sleep, how they do their chores, and so on.

The solution is not to completely ignore all of these issues. Instead, work on developing the understanding that your son or daughter has feelings and needs. Teenagers do need guidance, but not with an attitude of "you're a good-for-nothing." They need to know that you respect them and trust them.

People need about ten smiles a day in order to function at their maximum. Give your son or daughter frequent smiles, verbal greetings, waves, and acknowledgments through eye contact and in writing.

Small expressions of politeness such as "please," "thank you," "excuse me," "may I help," and "it's my pleasure," go a long way in promoting good will, peace, and harmony. It shows that you are considerate of other people's feelings. We all know how good we feel when people treat us with respect and courtesy.

Being able to admit the truth is one of the seven character traits of a wise person (*Avos* 5:7). Being able to apologize for an error and being able to say "I'm sorry" is essential for a wholesome relationship. Why? If you are a human being but you never seem to have an occasion to apologize, something is wrong. We all make mistakes occasionally. People will never feel comfortable with you if you can't be trusted to admit to the truth. You may be trying to save face for now, but in the long run you will lose a quality relationship.

We have a halachic obligation to apologize to people if we have hurt their feelings (*Orach Chaim* 606:1). This is especially important when dealing with teenagers. If you hurt your teenager with a hasty comment or an angry rebuke, you have to appease him or her, request forgiveness, and ask for another chance.

If your child breaks a rule or speaks disrespectfully, never bear a grudge against him, especially if he apologizes for what he has done. Your relationship will only be harmed if you refuse to forget his mistakes. Forgiving, on the other hand, is a kindness that stems from love. It demonstrates a willingness to reconnect and reestablish a relationship in a wholesome way.

As we mentioned above, coming to the defense of another is a form of loving him or her. This applies also when someone criticizes or gossips about your child when he or she is absent. We must demonstrate our love for our teenagers to the point that we refuse to tolerate negative comments about them.

We are all linked together. Hashem implanted

in us a natural love for our own children. However, we have to develop and nurture the relationship and make sure that our teenagers know that we love them, instead of feeling constantly harassed.

Say little and do much.

(*Avos* 1:15)

Talk is easy, but keeping your word is much more difficult. If you want your children to respect you, you have to stick by your word. Don't promise to do something for them if you know you won't be able to.

We have discussed several aspects of the obligation to love each other. But there is no end to this subject. We can expand our hearts and develop an attitude of acceptance and understanding toward our teenagers. There are many ways which we can help them and contribute to their lives.

The Torah sandwiches the mitzvah to rebuke others between "Do not hate your brother" and "Love your fellow Jew as yourself" (Vayikra 19:17–18). We may not ignore someone's negative, harmful, or destructive behavior. We do have a mitzvah of offering constructive criticism. But it must be preceded and followed by love, not hate. Before you deliver a criticism, tell your child sincerely how much you care about him or her. Your child must feel that you appreciate his or her intrinsic worth and potential greatness. You have to separate your teenager from his incorrect behavior. Do not attach a label to him. Let him know that you do not appreciate a specific behavior, but you do acknowledge his basic worth as an individual.

Mitzvos are not always easy to fulfill. We are tested in many ways. When people are difficult to deal with we are still expected to be kind to them. When someone offends you and then asks forgiveness, you are expected to grant it. Wouldn't you want someone to give you another chance if you had wronged him?

You have a responsibility to love others. You have to cultivate your feelings of love toward people, especially family members. Teenagers are a unique challenge because they are in a transition stage. They are maturing, growing more independent, and developing their unique personalities. At this crucial stage, they need more love and understanding than ever — no matter how difficult they are to get along with.

If you give in during an argument and avoid rubbing it in when you are obviously right, you are actually winning the battle, for you have fulfilled the mitzvah of loving others even when it is not easy. One component of loving others is generating an attitude that whatever is important to the other person is important to you also. Empathizing, sympathizing, and identifying with your teenagers is crucial.

Love will cover over all faults.

(Mishlei 10:12)

Compromises are a good way to demonstrate to your teenage son or daughter that you do care about his or her needs and that you expect him or her to care about yours.

Your teenager may need more freedom, a later curfew, more money, or new clothes. You may want him or her to help out at home, to strive for good grades, or to pick good friends. If both of you commit your expectations to paper and develop solutions that are acceptable to everyone, things will work out more smoothly for the two of you. Negotiating a peaceful agreement will give you both harmony in the home and reward in the next world (see *Shabbos* 127a).

You have to strive to understand each other, share your goals, clarify your expectations, commit yourself to the Torah and the mitzvos, and pray for heavenly assistance.

Priorities

You shall love Hashem, your God, with all your heart, with all your soul, and with all your possessions. Let these matters that I command you today be on your heart. Teach them diligently to your children and speak of them while you sit in your home, while you walk on the way, when you lie down [at night], and when you arise [in the morning].

(Devarim 6:5–7)

In these words of *Krias Shema*, which we recite twice a day, we declare our loyalty to Hashem and we recall our obligation to Him — in order of priority. We must love Hashem, put His words of Torah in our hearts, and teach them to our children.

Teaching our children is, therefore, one of the three top priorities in our lives.

Do you plan ahead to make sure to attend your son's *siyum*, or are you too busy and forget to put it on your calendar?

Do you sit with your child daily to help him review his Chumash lesson? And if you are there physically, is your mind there, too, or is it dwelling on other things?

A proper balance must be maintained with all that we juggle in our daily lives. We rationalize that we need to earn a living, and, since we send our children to good yeshivos, we do not really need to pay much attention to the progress our children are making in their studies. But this is wrong. As parents, we need to offer our children consistent emotional support and some intellectual stimulation to enhance their growth. We need to be constantly engaged in their growth and development.

If we were more determined to be there for our children, we would discover many creative avenues for encouraging and motivating them. The Gemara teaches that the command to "teach them diligently" means that the words of Torah should be sharp in your mouth through constant repetition and review (*Kiddushin* 30a). This is something that parents should particularly focus on. Find innovative, fun ways to help your child review.

> *You shall make them known to your children and grandchildren.*
>
> (Devarim 4:9)

What can be greater than nurturing a human being and helping him develop to his greatest potential?

It is absurd to think that we can absolve ourselves of our responsibility to our children if we find agents, albeit competent and caring ones, to work with our children in our stead. We add insult to injury if we neglect to follow up with our children's educators. The Gemara tells us that a sure way to lose your money quickly is to hire workers and not supervise them (*Bava Metzia* 29b). If this is true in the case of money, it is certainly true when it comes to our children.

Parents have to make their home a place of orderliness, harmony, and good cheer. When a parent learns with his children, speaks to them, listens to them, and spends time relaxing with them, the children feel loved. This is an atmosphere which will encourage them to thrive.

Ultimately, the goal of parenting is not merely to direct and tell children what to do, but rather to train them to become independently observant Jews, to be self-motivated. Teach the Torah principles to your children so that they will be able to speak about them on their own.

We have to keep asking ourselves, Who is raising our children? When we do not invest enough effort in our families, the destructive atmosphere of the outside world penetrates, corrodes, and corrupts.

One of the sources which teach us the importance of the family is the following verse in *Megillas Esther*: "These days should be remembered and celebrated in every generation, by every family" (Esther 9:28). The verse does not say, "by every person," but rather "by every family." The home teaches and facilitates good virtues, values, and standards. The family unit is the foundation of the support structure of Judaism and the glue that holds things together.

Children need role models. They need authority, support, advice, and guidance. Parents are vital for filling all of these needs.

The Torah provides guidelines, structure, and priorities which make a family healthy and stable. We learn how to treat each other and care for each other. We are also blessed with opportunities to spend time together as a family. The three Shabbos meals, for example, allow families to bond. The support and strength you give your children at the Shabbos table supply them with fond memories that last a lifetime.

We may be busy all week long, but on Shabbos we must take the time to share life-sustaining principles with our family. We must teach our children lessons from the parashah and lessons from life that focus on the joys of Judaism. We can discuss challenges in life and how to deal with them one step at a time.

It is important for parents to plan these family togetherness sessions. Perhaps invite guests to join you and share their experiences. Learn how they have reached their goals.

Review the highlights of your child's week and

discuss issues and problems which may have come up. Sing *zemiros* together to round out the picture and provide for the emotional and spiritual needs of your children.

Cultivate a sense of fun and excitement for your children to ensure that each one participates and enjoys the learning experiences. Again, this takes planning and creativity, but it is well worth the time and effort.

Having fun times together unites the family. But we should not ignore the mitzvah aspects of these fun times. Try to develop in your family a sense of joy for mitzvos, one which will hopefully last for the rest of their lives.

Besides family time together, parents need to recognize each child as a unique individual and periodically spend time alone with him or her. Giving each child his turn for private time shows that you really care about him, you are eager to listen to him, and you love him.

Your undivided attention is the greatest gift to a spouse or child. During this private time, refrain from any criticism. Listen with caring and concern.

Do not offer any advice unless you are specifically asked for it.

In order for your children to learn how to live a happy, fulfilled, Torah life, they have to feel comfortable with you. They have to feel that you love them unconditionally. Once you have forged a solid relationship with them, discipline can be administered more effectively. Building a firm relationship when your children are young and constantly strengthening it as they mature will spare you from a great amount of troubles later on.

Your relationships with your family require constant attention, maintenance, and reevaluation. We tend to take loved ones for granted, while strangers will receive a lion's share of our consideration. This is wrong. Although it is true that all people deserve to be honored, a special devotion must be reserved solely for our family members. They must be valued above all others: appreciate them, acknowledge them, express love for them, and apologize profusely when you wrong them.

Chapter Six

Understanding Others

Acquire for yourself a friend and judge every person meritoriously.

(*Avos* 1:6)

W hat is the link between friendship and how we judge others?

Every person views the world and the people around him through his own eyes. His perception filters through his life experiences, his upbringing, and his training. For this reason, we often have difficulty relating to and communicating with others, which often results in misunderstandings and dissension.

Real understanding leads to friendships that are attachments of value. "*Acquire* for yourself a friend" means take action to create a bond, an attachment. We have to be patient with one another and learn to be sensitive to each individual's unique way of looking at things. When we do this, we will not find it difficult to judge others in a positive light.

In the first *mishnah* of *Pirkei Avos* we are taught: "Be patient in judgement and teach many disciples." These two lessons are also linked together. If you are not hasty to judge others, you will be successful in teaching many people.

We must tune in to the many different ways of perceiving things and to different definitions for the same words. The "pause-power" lesson is vital here — take the time to understand what people are going through before you judge them.

> *The words of the wise, when spoken gently, are accepted.*
>
> (Koheles 9:17)

People who shout and yell are attempting to say, "Listen to me! Respect me!" However, the approach is erroneous. You'll find that the results are anything but what you desire. When you shout at your family members, they won't accept what you are saying. Instead, they become defensive and annoyed, which only exacerbates the problem.

Everyone desires to be understood. We all yearn for recognition and appreciation. Speaking gently to your spouse and children is a sign that you do recognize their intrinsic worth, their unique contribution. When treated kindly, they will respond the same way and accept your message.

A person should never impose excessive fear upon his household.

(*Gittin* 6b)

If you are pleasant and agreeable most of the time, but on occasion you blow your stack and demonstrate a vicious temper, it will affect your family even when everything is calm. Family members will constantly be afraid that your anger might explode again. They will withdraw and refuse to communicate with you in a completely honest way.

If you have lashed out uncontrollably in the past, the solution is to first acknowledge your loss of control. Second, apologize and procure forgiveness from your victims. Finally, take precautions against a recurrence: learn how to overcome or, better yet, avoid your anger and learn to express yourself in a more productive and healthy way. (For further discussion of this topic, see our book *Guard Your Anger* [Southfield: Targum/Feldheim 1999].)

The Torah stresses that you should "love your friend as yourself." What does it mean to love others exactly as we love ourselves?

Think about your deepest desires and ambitions for a few minutes. Have you ever shared these with others? Think about how others view you and how you view yourself. Does anyone really know you, besides Hashem?

Each one of us pretends many things. We all wear many masks and hats that we interchange as situations dictate. We act as if we are secure, confident, and calm. Deep inside, we may be confused, fearful, and lonely.

We can love others more truthfully once we acquire an awareness of ourselves. As we recognize the silent voice inside ourselves, we can be more empathetic to the silent cry that emanates from each person we encounter.

Listening is an important tool. When someone wants to talk to us, the biggest *chesed* we can do for him or her is listen. We often attempt to advise people who come to confide in us — though they might not want any advice. They would appreciate it more if we would strive to understand their needs.

Ask yourself, "Am I trying to help, or am I merely waiting for the opportunity to interject my ideas or experience?" Try to understand the speaker and convey the fact that you understand. You may not need to say anything at all — facial expressions filled with compassion may be sufficient. Empathize with the person in need and be aware of his expressions, tone of voice, and emotional state. When your spouse or child knows you care, that makes all the difference in the world.

Chapter Seven

Thinking of Others

*Do not appease your friend while he is angry....
Do not attempt to see him while he is
downcast.*

(Avos 4:23)

One indication of a person who is truly sensitive to the needs of others is that he knows when to keep his distance and when to come close. Some parents make their children very uncomfortable by prying into their lives excessively. Others never involve themselves at all. Good parenting requires a balance — and the foresight to know what is appropriate when.

When a person feels threatened, trying to instruct him will cause resentment. If your child or teenager is depressed, realize that it is not the best time to offer constructive criticism. Wait until he is in a more receptive frame of mind. By withholding your comments until then, you are communicating respect and understanding to your child. On the other hand, if you try to lecture him, he will feel even more threatened and misunderstood. You need to express your affection, respect, and esteem for him more than anything else.

You cannot teach a person how to swim when he is drowning. All he wants is a helping hand or a rope. Your support, until the pressure or depression lifts, is the most important thing at that point.

In general, it is important to keep timing in mind before you deliver criticism. You have to know when to have fun and when to be more serious. When you have family togetherness time, your children should enjoy themselves. It is not the time and place for judging and disciplining the children.

On Shabbos, for example, you want everyone present to enjoy the day and spend time together in a relaxed and calm atmosphere. Children should not perceive Shabbos as the day when their parents have more time to yell at them!

When people disagree with one another they

try to prove their point of view, no matter what. This is a lack of respect to the other person and usually does not accomplish much. Try this instead: Do not state your own view until you first make sure you understand the other person's point. This, the Gemara (*Eiruvin* 13b) teaches, was the secret greatness of Hillel and his disciples: they would always study their opponents' opinions first, and then they would continue with their own opinions. For this reason, we usually follow the opinion of Bais Hillel.

Rav Chaim Shmuelevitz explains that this is extremely beneficial for a very logical reason: When you listen to and work to understand your opponent's view, you will be more prepared to explain your angle to the situation, and you will expand your argument to take into account the opposing view. After you have shown respect for the other person (whether he or she is your spouse, your child, or anyone else) by listening to his view, and you have clearly explained your own view, it will be much easier to reach an agreement.

Two are better than one.

(Koheles 4:9)

When you learn with a *chavrusa* (study partner), you will always gain more than you will when learning by yourself. The exchange of ideas increases the creativity, stimulates your mind, and makes your learning experience more joyful and exciting. The two of you will also develop a greater camaraderie, resulting in a total win/win arrangement.

The same is true when you need to develop a solution to a problem in your family. When you strive for mutual respect and understanding, you will have input from both parties, enabling you to discover new solutions that are better for everyone. Both parties will be motivated to accept the solution when they have some part in creating it.

However, this calls for more open-mindedness and humility, a greater willingness to learn and change. You must be careful not to resent the other person's views or input. Rather, appreciate, value, and even rejoice with the differences in personality and style because they enhance the final solution.

When you both contribute your strengths to tackle the issue and you both take turns listening to each other, you can have your eyes opened to a whole new way of seeing things. Your sharing of ideas will lead to a much greater understanding of the whole topic. For example, if one of you is excellent at understanding the overall concept, while the other is able to grasp every fine detail, then you have two parts of a greater whole. Unified, you create a deeper understanding.

A problem in a family can be utilized to develop an overall better relationship. Turn it into a growth experience. It should encourage you to develop yourself in different areas. For example, if a child poses difficulties, use it as an opportunity to work on your patience and calm. Instead of complaining and criticizing, learn to appreciate the benefits that result from problems.

> *Do not desire your friend's house...his wife, his servants...or anything else that he possesses.*
> (Shemos 20:14)

This teaches us to avoid comparing and competing. "Who is wealthy? He who rejoices with his portion" (*Avos* 4:1). Your portion includes your spouse, car, house, clothing, job, and even your problems in life. Hashem gave you this wife and these children at this time in your life because they will help you develop your potential to its maximum.

Prayer to Hashem is necessary at all times and for every occasion. We should ask Hashem to help us to listen more effectively to other people, perceive the true issues of a problem, determine the ideal solution, and implement it. When we ask Hashem for help, we know that we are not alone.

Chapter Eight

Maintaining Relationships

How do you create a lasting bond with your family members?

The first step is to develop mutual respect and work on creative cooperation. When you interact with your spouse and children, the primary goal should always be to exhibit respect and caring. You have to train yourself to really listen and to consider the underlying needs, feelings, and fears of your spouse and children. The foundation of a good relationship is a cooperative spirit, not a desire to fill your own needs.

Any love that is dependent on something, when that thing is gone, the love will be gone. Any [love] that is not dependent on a thing will not cease forever.

(Avos 5:19)

You may rely on your spouse to provide for you financially or to cook, clean, and do the laundry. But the *mishnah* teaches that money or possessions will not bring about an enduring relationship. They may provide some temporary satisfaction, but they are not enough for an ideal lifetime relationship. Enduring love and happiness results from a relationship that is based on caring and respect. At times we may have differences of opinion, but when we deal with them with mutual respect the issues can be resolved diplomatically and positively.

Any dispute that is for the sake of Heaven will have a constructive outcome, but one that is not for the sake of Heaven will not have a constructive outcome.

(Ibid., 20)

If your goal is to fulfill Hashem's will, you will seek to understand the opposing viewpoint and agree to compromise if need be. Ego will not play a part in your argument and tempers will not rise if the issue is how will our family best serve Hashem.

It is no coincidence that the concepts of lasting love and disputing for the sake of Heaven are juxtaposed in the Mishnah. When you have a relationship based on caring and respect, instead of on external objects, you can keep in mind your true goals even when you disagree.

Focus on recognizing the positive aspects of your family members. When you interact with your spouse or children, think, *You are of infinite worth; there is no one who can compare to you. You are unique. I value you and love you. I will always be there to cherish you and support you as much as possible.*

Tune in to the specific reasons that make your spouse or child endearing and special. Whether they are significant or insignificant reasons, they help us appreciate our family members properly. For example, if your husband expresses himself clearly, fixes everything, or is good with the children; if your wife is a great cook, good organizer, or smooths over arguments; if your child is creative, helpful in the home, and diligent, these are all things which should engender admiration and love in you.

Even the best relationship will disintegrate and people will drift apart if there are no ongoing efforts to maintain and develop it.

Four things require fortification: Torah, good deeds, prayer, and derech eretz (good manners).

(Berachos 32b)

Just like we have to be careful not to neglect our bodies, homes, and cars, we also need to pay attention to our relationships. The good deeds or the *chesed* that we do for our family members, as well as the *derech eretz* we must display for them, require constant attention and strengthening. We need to renew our relationships and ourselves regularly.

We learn from our physical needs about our spiritual needs — just as we need to energize ourselves physically by eating three meals a day, we need to energize ourselves spiritually by davening three times a day to Hashem. We also need to regularly strengthen our relationships with one another by providing services to others, giving tzedakah, learning and teaching.

When families learn Torah together and share

ideas that they have heard, they gain in many ways as they create a close family bond. When they go to daven together or celebrate Shabbos and *yom tov*, they are strengthening their relationship as well as their faith. They become more connected through proclaiming and repeating lessons that are important to them all.

The monthly times when a husband and wife renew their relationship with each other goes a long way in showing how important their relationship is to them. When you invest time and patience, respect and thought for another person, you develop an ongoing, maturing relationship.

The family unit provides many opportunities to do mitzvos for other people. We nurture each other, love and care for each other, and respect and honor each other. For our children, we provide a feeling of belonging, support, and understanding. All this requires dedication and commitment, but it is all worth it.

The Torah provides us with a weekly opportunity to spend time with our family: Shabbos. We should put much effort into the Shabbos table in order for it to be an enjoyable and meaningful event for the whole family. In this way, we show our spouses and our children that we love them and want to do good for them.

One way to make Shabbos more personal for every family member is to give everyone a specific job he or she can do to prepare for Shabbos. Let each child have a job that is suitable for him and make sure it is something he will enjoy. This way, each person will feel he has a part in Shabbos and in helping the family out. The Gemara teaches us that the great Sages would personally participate in preparations for Shabbos by doing specific tasks every Friday (*Shabbos* 119a).

Another mitzvah which should be done actively as a family is reciting *Birkas HaMazon*. When the family *bentches* together, we are reminded to be grateful to Hashem for our food, our lives, our Torah, and everything else we have.

Besides Shabbos, we have two special weeks in the year, Pesach and Sukkos, which remind us of our privileged status as Hashem's nation and give us spiritual energy which lasts until the next *yom tov*.

Hashem desires that we celebrate these days with enthusiasm. Every *yom tov* is a time of renewal, to relive history and recommit ourselves to Hashem, His Torah, and the mitzvos. When the family gets together to celebrate, they can be inspired and uplifted together, bringing everyone closer to Hashem.

Each *yom tov* has its mitzvah themes that reoccur every year. Thus, it is easy to create a sense of anticipation around them.

At the splitting of the Yam Suf, the Jewish nation declared, "This is my God and I will adorn Him" (Shemos 15:2). This means that we must beautify Hashem's mitzvos (*Shabbos* 133a). We may be celebrating *yom tov* in a routine way, failing to appreciate more of its significance. It pays to study the concepts, themes, and lessons of each *yom tov* in order to inspire ourselves and our families to celebrate with more enthusiasm.

There are many opportunities for families to learn together in a fun way. Teach your family to enjoy singing *zemiros*, learn new songs, and brush up on old favorites. Teach your children to understand the Torah values of the *zemiros* you sing, most of which are based on the teachings of our Sages.

Why not share the meaning of the Shabbos *zemiros* and the meaning of the daily, Shabbos, and *yom tov* prayers with your family? You will help them to be inspired by these principles, and you will all enjoy singing and davening more. No matter what Torah activities you choose to involve yourselves in, as long as you make it fun for your children, your relationship with them will be strengthened.

Chapter Nine

Showing You Care

How can you make your family's life more pleasant? By showing that you care about them. When your spouse or children come home at the end of a long day, greet them warmly, ask them about their day, and talk things over. By concentrating on their needs, you will enrich your relationship immensely. Focusing on someone by asking questions and listening to the answers demonstrates that you desire to be involved in his life and daily activities.

People feel good when they sense that you missed them. They feel assured that you consider them to be an important part of the family. Show that you love to spend time with them by smiling and putting enthusiasm into your greeting.

It is a relatively easy mitzvah to smile at others.

There are many opportunities that come our way daily to fulfill the following *mishnah*:

> Greet every person with a pleasant, interested face [sever panim yafos].

(*Avos* 1:15)

Although this seems to be a simple, straightforward direction, a close examination will reveal that there is much we can learn from it. Rav Avigdor Miller explains that there are three parts to this directive (*Sing, You Righteous*, p. 291):

1. The word *sever* (interested) is similar to *svara*, which denotes thought and interest. Show that you care about the person.

2. *Panim* (face) — turn your whole face to greet the person, and show that your entire focus is on them.

3. *Yafos* (pleasant) — Make sure your countenance is bright and pleasant.

> In the behavior we use toward others, Hashem behaves toward us.

(*Sotah* 8b)

Hashem shines His face on those whose faces

shine on others. Rashi on the above Gemara says Hashem smiles and radiates His countenance to us.

When we smile, we fulfill the great mitzvah which is considered the foundation of all of the mitzvos of the Torah: "Love your fellow Jew as yourself" (Vayikra 19:18), for everyone desires to be received with a smile.

Toras Avraham records that Rav Avraham Grodzensky, *zt"l*, spent two years practicing and perfecting this art of greeting others with a pleasant countenance.

The warmth of a smile can light up a person's day. Every person needs encouragement, even one who is independent and self-confident, and especially those who tend to be discouraged. We have to learn from the beautiful flowers that Hashem puts in this world to gladden a person's heart. By honoring those whom we encounter with a pleasant countenance, we bring happiness to the world and emulate Hashem. A smile can brighten every situation.

Reb Yochanan teaches that one who shows his white teeth to others (in a smile) is better than one who provides them milk to drink (*Kesubos* 111b). What a great benefit milk is! It provides nourishment for the body, enabling the recipient to live and function. A smile is even greater. It elevates the mood and spirit of the recipient, giving him encouragement and the drive to live and function.

Every parent provides milk for his children daily, but does he think about providing regular smiles?

By loving our fellow Jews who are created in Hashem's image and who are His children, we are also expressing our love of Hashem. The Mishnah teaches, "Your friend's honor should be as dear to you as your own" (*Avos* 2:10). We should always try to treat others the way we desire to be treated.

Our Sages teach us that when a person passes away, he will be asked the following questions (*Reishis Chochmah, Shaar HaYirah* 12):

❖ Did you study Torah?

❖ Were you involved in acts of kindness?

❖ Did you proclaim Hashem as your King morning and evening?

❖ Did you treat your friends as if they were kings over you?

We see a parallel between honoring Hashem and honoring our fellow people. Although we may sometimes be very busy, we are not allowed to ignore our obligations to Hashem — we must still make time for praying and learning Torah daily. In the same way, we are not allowed to ignore our obligation to treat our family members with respect, care, and concern.

People occasionally get so wrapped up in their mitzvos and service of Hashem that they forget about the people in their lives. This is a grave error. No matter what we are involved in, we cannot hurt the feelings of our family members.

Rav Yisrael Salanter, *zt"l*, related how one *erev Yom Kippur*, as he was going to shul to daven *maariv*, he encountered a great, God-fearing Jew who was enveloped in a fear of the Day of Atonement. Reb Yisrael asked him a question but received no response.

As he walked away, he thought to himself, *Why do I have to suffer because you desire to be a pious person? Aren't you obligated to respond to my question out of courtesy and chesed?*

Let us make sure that our families never think the same thing about us!

Pirkei Avos teaches further: "Greet every person with joy" (*Avos* 3:16).

This is an even higher level than a smile. Every person in your home needs your smile — but you also have to develop an inner joy to go along with it. As our inner joy develops, our smile also becomes brighter, happier, and warmer. People will love to be with you and feel elevated by the glow that emanates from you. Have you ever seen a child who lights up when you enter the room? Don't you love that type of reaction?

Make your family feel that your smile is unique for them. Try saying, "Ahhh, it's so-and-so, the world's greatest son or daughter!" and watch your child's face brighten. And don't stop with the greeting. Your child should feel that you are really there for him or her.

"Be the first to greet every person" (*Avos* 4:15). *Alei Shur* (1:190) explains that this is a form of sunshine that we radiate toward others.

When you walk outside into the beautiful sunshine and you notice the freshness of a new morning, you feel invigorated and refreshed. Try to spread this kind of sunshine to your family every morning and evening. Just as plants cannot exist without sunshine, children and adults cannot develop without the ongoing nurturing of smiling faces around them.

A genuine smile begins in the heart and mind and engages the eyes, the lips, and the entire face. Your smile can improve the world and leave a lasting impact on everyone you meet. Most of all, though, you should use it to bring joy to your family members and to your life.

Chapter Ten

Small Principles

The best way to bring about changes in your family life is to take things slowly. Implement a plan that calls for small steps, easily accomplished. For example, you can:

1. Commit yourself to spending five minutes more a day with your children, reviewing their schoolwork or talking about events of the day.

2. Decide not to criticize your teenager for one week, giving yourself a chance to prove how much you love him or her.

3. Choose a ten-minute period every day to practice staying calm.

4. Pick one family member to smile at and greet affectionately every day.

Do you want to revolutionize your family? You can do it. Every person has the capacity to change the entire world, as Avraham Avinu did, but the starting point is himself.

It may take you a while to commit yourself wholeheartedly to a project, no matter what it is. We all have fears and doubts. *Do I have what it takes to follow through? Can I handle the pressure?* We are scared that we may fail. It is normal to experience trepidation when faced with life's challenges.

"On the path one is determined to go, he will be led" (*Makos* 10b). Hashem is always there for us, waiting for us to make the total commitment. We have to make a supreme effort to do our best in communicating with our family, and Hashem will help us at that point. You will begin to notice small improvements and then big ones.

When you achieve a small victory in controlling yourself, you become stronger (*Avos* 4:1). As you change and improve yourself, others, especially your family, will be influenced from your example.

When you set goals and strive to achieve them,

you are becoming stronger. When you do even small acts of kindness regularly, you enjoy them, others are happy, and you become an elevated person.

The most important thing to recognize is that everything in life is a choice.

A person's foolishness corrupts his path, but he gets angry at Hashem.

(Mishlei 19:3)

We often think the bad situations we end up in are Hashem's "fault." This is a mistake — we are responsible to a large extent for the events in our lives and how we deal with them.

Your choice to take responsibility for your attitude in all situations can be the most profitable decision you make in your life. You can take the initiative to change your behavior patterns, to improve your family life, and to succeed. You can stop your bad habits, learn good ones, and eventually teach them to others.

❖ You choose whether or not to get angry.

❖ You choose to take charge, to be responsible.

❖ You can choose to remain calm, cool, and in control.

❖ You choose to enjoy the weather.

❖ You choose to laugh.

❖ You choose your attitude.

❖ You choose whether or not to be happy.

Happiness depends mostly on your attitude. You can train yourself to perceive every day as a happy occasion.

Everything that Hashem does is for the good.
(Berachos 60b)

Our plans don't always come to fruition the way we expected them to, but we can make minor adjustments and go on to celebrate the "good" that Hashem always sends our way. Don't feel sorry for yourself, feel happy! Don't miss out on all that Hashem wants you to enjoy (For more on this topic, please see our book *Master Your Thoughts* [Southfield: Targum/Feldheim, 2000].)

Every family has imperfect people, complicated relationships, and unfortunate circumstances. Celebrations don't always turn out the way we anticipate they will, but when we accept Hashem's good, we can find even greater happiness.

We have to learn to appreciate the family and friends Hashem has surrounded us with. Then we will be able to enjoy life in all of its phases.

Each family member is a gift to us from Hashem, who knows what our personality is like and what we need to succeed. How can you deal with a particularly difficult family member? The answer is it's a choice. *You* can choose to make your mother-in-law like a second mother. *You* can decide to get along with your moody teenager. Relationships aren't automatic; they're a process that we develop over time with work and commitment.

How can you build a bonding connection with someone? Spending time together daily is essential. Your presence is one of the most powerful forms of communication. It says to the person, "You are very important to me! You and your interests are a priority for me, and I don't want to miss your significant events or activities."

You may not consider your son's game important as an activity, but when you spend time playing it with him, he understands that his importance has transformed it into a meaningful and enjoyable event.

The Hebrew word for family, *mishpachah*, has a similar root to the word *shofech* (to pour). We tend to think of our family members as a chance of the draw, the luck of the dice. The truth is, however, that it is a most precise arrangement by the Master of all living beings. We have to learn to nurture our family connections and realize how precious they are. Hashem has "poured" you, so to speak, into a family blend that has tremendous potential.

When you capitalize on the treasures Hashem surrounds you with, your very own family members, you will be able to enjoy life more. Appreciate the uniqueness of each family member. Work on defining the purposes of your lives together, encouraging and building each other's self-esteem. Develop better communication skills, train yourself to speak less *lashon hara* and verbal abuse, and focus on forgiveness and trust.

We often judge our family members quickly without having all the facts about a certain situation.

Why are they acting in a certain way? What is their point of view? To really communicate with others, you have to learn to keep an open mind about their actions. Do not expect them to always act the way you would.

One of the most useful keys to dealing effectively with people and avoiding problematic confrontations is what we call the "win/win" solution.

We tend to enjoy winning an argument — being right and proving that our adversary is absolutely wrong. This inclination causes tension and bitter feelings between us and our spouses, our children, and whoever we need to deal with.

Break yourself of this bad habit by saying to yourself, "Let me do this person a favor and allow him the final word this time." Try to understand his point of view and cooperate with him, so that tension does not build up.

One who overlooks insults is forgiven for all of his sins.

(Rosh HaShanah 17a)

When you allow the other person to win, you become the winner in Hashem's eyes. When we reach out to the other person by endeavoring to understand his needs and concerns, we are performing a tremendous *chesed*, and, what is more, we are emulating Hashem's ways. Measure for measure, Hashem will forgive us for our shortcomings toward Him.

However, this is not to suggest that you turn into a martyr who allows everyone to step on him. Respect for others has limits; do not forgo the respect your children should have for you (and others). Bear in mind, though, that the primary concern should not be *who* is right, but *what* is right.

For petty issues that are only a matter of preference, it always pays to let others have their way. When you let them win in matters of little or no consequence, they will admire you more for it, and most likely they will be prepared to follow your lead when it comes to issues that are significant to you.

When you give in during an argument and avoid rubbing it in when you are obviously right, you really win, for you have fulfilled the mitzvah of loving others even when it is not easy.

Chapter Eleven

Family Wholesomeness

There are many components to the successful running of a healthy Torah home. Among them are caring for the physical needs of the family, infusing the home with positive energy, and avoiding negative energy like envy, hatred, or lust. A support base of like-minded, friendly people who aim to grow spiritually is paramount. The family must be unified in order for each of the members to deal with difficulties, setbacks, and everyday challenges of life in a meaningful, Torah-guided way.

The definition of a Jewish family's mission has to be reiterated regularly: "The world stands on three pillars: Torah, service, and kindness" (*Avos* 1:2).

The Mishnah (*Avos*, ch. 1) describes the home as a learning center and as a center of kindness to all. We are in this world to emulate the Creator. Thus, we must learn and teach His ways and practice *chesed* toward family members and others.

Each of us can make a difference in the lives of others and be a shining light to the world. One of the greatest ways of helping others is to help them see the best in themselves. Help your spouse and your children to tap into their infinite potential. A significant part of a person's development happens in the family setting.

Parents should guide and direct their children in all three areas of life — Torah learning, service of Hashem (davening), and doing *chesed*. Involve your children in specific forms of *chesed* such as caring for a grandparent, dealing with a handicapped neighbor, assisting children who have trouble in school, fund-raising, and so on. Projects like these can teach all of the participants many valuable lessons and can give them something to be proud of and feel fulfilled from. When you live to serve others, you become energized, satisfied, and fulfilled.

When a family works together to serve Hashem, each family member grows and learns to serve Hashem in a more effective manner. A family together can make a greater difference in the world than each individual can by himself.

A family can achieve greatness when they realize that Hashem is behind them. He has put them together for the benefit of each individual and for the family as a whole.

Each member of a family has the potential to help the entire family grow. We all learn from each other, whether we like it or not. What we see or do not see influences us. When children see decent behavior and integrity, they will want to emulate that form of behavior. Everyone learns more from examples than from verbal messages. A parent's real desires, values, and beliefs are conveyed more through his behavior than through his speech. Your children will pick up on your values, good and bad alike, and emulate your behavior.

When spouses fight regularly, when they handle differences and disagreements in unpleasant ways, their children learn to quarrel and fight, too. Every behavior children witness shapes their thinking. A sharp exchange will teach them that raised voices are acceptable; kind words will teach them how to deal kindly with others. Parents serve as the primary role models of their children. Everything you do is inscribed in their young minds and hearts forever (*Avos* 4:25).

If we want to be proper role models, we must analyze our lives and our behavior.

❖ Am I a proud Jew?

❖ Do I live my life according to the Torah?

❖ Do I demonstrate love and respect for others?

❖ Do I practice self-control and discipline?

❖ Do I watch what I say?

❖ Do I interrupt others while they are speaking?

❖ Do I rush to respond without trying to understand the speaker?

❖ Do I admit to the truth when I am wrong?

You are your children's first source of physical and emotional security. You care for them and love them deeply. Do they know you love them or do they feel rejected by you? They won't listen to your teachings if they feel that you do not really care about them.

How can you show you care? Moshe Rabbeinu left Pharaoh's palace to see the plight of his brethren (Shemos 2:11). Going out of your way to look at someone's situation is the first step. Rashi explains that Moshe focused his eyes and his heart to sympathize with the enslaved Jews. In addition, Moshe helped his brethren in a physical way. This is the second step — besides offering words of encouragement and appreciation, one should be willing to sacrifice for others, caring and serving them. We must also pray for others when they need help.

A Jewish parent's main job is to train his or her children to follow the way of the Torah. This involves occasional rebuke and discipline. The Torah teaches us an important principle with the command, "Rebuke your *fellow* Jew (Vayikra 19:17) — a person will only accept your message if you treat him cordially and kindly.

To get people to have an open ear and mind to your criticism, they need to see you care about them. Your words will simply deflect off your children if you do not build and maintain proper relationships with them. If they feel you love and care for them, they will value themselves more and become more open to your influence.

It is important to keep in mind the Mishnah's instruction: "Say a little and do a lot" (*Avos* 1:18). Talk is cheap. Some people frequently talk about doing things with their family and showing how much they love them, but then, when it comes down to it, they are always too busy to do anything with them. We learn from Moshe Rabbeinu that we have to involve ourselves and act on love.

Show that your family is truly important to you by having meals together, sharing your day with each person, and spending leisure time together. Your family will develop a sense of security and structure. When you do something with your child that he enjoys, he becomes receptive to your input and you develop a bond that is essential in parenting.

If we do not reach out to love and teach our children, society fills that void, and family tragedy may result, Heaven forbid.

Whether you realize it or not, your family learns from how you set goals, how you treat others, and especially how you value your family. When you show your children how much you love them, they will learn to value themselves.

Parents sometimes get their priorities confused, spending time on other things when they should be spending time with their children. For example, if a father remains late in shul Friday night or Shabbos morning in order to catch up on his learning, having his children walk home by themselves, there may be something wrong. It is not wrong to learn Torah, but walking home together from shul should take priority.

In *Krias Shema*, it does not merely say, "Teach your children always." Rather, it says, "You shall speak of them when you in your home, while you walk on the way, when you lie down, and when you arise" (Devarim 6:7). We are servants of Hashem, and we are required to teach our children to live with His Torah, in all circumstances.

When one member of the family increases the amount of Torah he learns or expends more effort for mitzvos, each of the members of the family benefits. Every person has many roles to play in life, enabling him to develop his potential in many different areas. By setting a good example in all that you do, you are building up your children. They will learn from you to excel in all areas of their lives.

Every child is unique and poses a particular challenge to the parents. Some children are full of energy, and need to be taught how to channel it properly; others are very shy and need to be encouraged to come out of their shells. A father and mother need to combine forces to unlock the capabilities and potential of each of their children.

When your children hit rough spots in their development, realize that it is a test from Hashem for you as well — an opportunity to develop your child and yourself.

Hashem has given you the responsibility to take care of yourself and your family. Your role is to care and provide for your sons and daughters in both the material and spiritual realms. Lead your children and train them to avoid the negative and welcome the positive. By sharing aspirations, goals, and dreams you can inspire your children to grow and excel in life.

Recognize that you can become a strong role model. You can become more involved with your children. You can devote more time and energy to them. You can encourage them to set important goals in Torah and in other areas of life. You can help them overcome any obstacles and build a positive future. You can make a profound influence on the lives of all your family members.

It will take effort on your part. You need to develop the attitude that you are capable of doing it. The Mishnah teaches that you were created in Hashem's image and that you are a child of Hashem (*Avos* 3:18). When you accept who you are and live as you should, you will inspire others.

You can do it, with Hashem's help.

Think Win/Win

If you face your ongoing challenges with prayer, work to understand others, and then set goals that are beneficial for everyone involved, you will succeed in whatever you set out to accomplish. You need to focus on the priorities in life.

A family consists of individual members. Recognize the value of each family member and ask yourself periodically, "How can I serve this family that Hashem blessed me with?" Pray for each person and think about what you can do for him or her. Perhaps you can designate one day of the week to each member of the family.

To facilitate success, look at the following list of questions that will help you tackle the issues as they arise:

1. What should my goals be now?

2. How should I tackle my goals?

3. How can I help my spouse or child achieve as I attend to my own needs?

4. Am I praying sincerely to Hashem *Yisbarach* for His help?

> *Be bold and courageous as a leopard…to do the will of your Father in Heaven.*
>
> (Avos 5:20)

We are all part of Hashem's family. He is our Heavenly Father and we have to dedicate our lives to fulfill His desires above all else. When we are patient, persistent, kind, cheerful, and courageous, we are fulfilling His desire. All these are essential in creating and nurturing a warm home environment. We have to realize that Hashem will help us when we energize ourselves to perform His mitzvos.

What makes us who we are? Our Sages refer to us as the "descendants of Avraham, Yitzchak, and Yaakov." When we learn about our ancestors and study how they lived, struggled, and triumphed, we will be inspired to follow in their footsteps. Like our ancestors, we will leave a legacy to our descendants. Our family legacy inspires us to reach into the depths of our souls and try to follow the way of life of our forefathers.

Hashem will help us build our family when we take the initiative to do all that is within our power.

The real focus of each person's life should be to please Hashem by learning Torah, performing mitzvos, and developing one's potential. This goal is unchangeable and timeless. When we keep this focus in mind, we will recognize our family as one of our top priorities. Some people become consumed by work or hobbies, losing all equilibrium. This is extremely detrimental to their family life. When we stay focused on Torah, this will not happen to us.

If you apply the Torah's principles to your life, it will become more wholesome. Your home should be a place of love of Hashem, love of people, love of work, honesty, respect, and gratitude. Your family will gain the most from life when the home is based on these principles.